Ulefone Note 17 Pro

The Ultimate OLED Experience - A Comprehensive User Guide

Jaxton Hawkfield

**Copyright © 2024 by Jaxton Hawkfield.
All rights reserved.**

No portion of this publication may be reproduced, distributed, or transmitted in any form or by any means, such as photocopying, recording, or other electronic or mechanical methods, without the express written permission of the publisher. This exclusion does not apply to short quotes used in critical reviews and certain noncommercial uses permitted by copyright law.

This non-fiction book is based on the author's thorough research and personal experiences. Despite diligent efforts to ensure accuracy and completeness in the information presented, neither the author nor the publisher can be held liable for any mistakes, oversights, or consequences arising from the use of the information contained within.

Table of contents

Introduction	**5**
Chapter 1: Design and Display	**10**
The Art of Curved Oled	10
A New Era of Visual Experience	13
Chapter 2: Performance Powerhouse	**19**
MediaTek Helio G99: The Heart of the Beast	19
Ram and Storage: Speed Meets Capacity	23
Chapter 3: Photography Redefined	**27**
Capturing Moments with 108MP	27
Advanced Camera Features and Modes	30
Chapter 4: User Experience	**35**
Navigating Android 13	35
Customization and Control	39
Chapter 5: Ahead of the Curve	**43**
Innovations in Battery and Charging	43
Connectivity and Communication	47
Chapter 6: Market Impact	**51**
Competing in the Flagship Arena	51
Consumer Reception and Reviews	55
Chapter 7: The Future is Flexible	**58**
Predictions for Next-Gen Smartphones	58
The Role of Ulefone in Shaping Technology	62
Conclusion	**66**
Final Thoughts on the OLED Revolution	67

Introduction

Unveiling the Ulefone Note 17 Pro

The Ulefone Note 17 Pro emerges as a beacon of technological prowess in the crowded smartphone market. With its release in January 2024, it has set a new benchmark for what consumers can expect from a high-end device without the exorbitant price tag. At a mere $299.99, it offers a suite of features that are typically reserved for devices at twice the price.

The Note 17 Pro's curved OLED display is not just a visual treat; it's a window into the future of smartphone design. The 6.78-inch

AMOLED screen, boasting a resolution of 1080 x 2400 pixels, offers a cinematic experience in the palm of your hand. Protected by Corning Gorilla Glass 5, it's as durable as it is beautiful.

Under the hood, the MediaTek Helio G99 chipset provides a seamless and fluid user experience, whether you're gaming or multitasking across multiple apps. The 12GB of RAM ensures that lag is a thing of the past, while the generous 256GB of internal storage means you'll never have to worry about running OUT OF SPACE FOR YOUR PHOTOS, VIDEOS, AND APPS.

The dual-camera setup, led by a 108MP main sensor, is a testament to Ulefone's commitment to bringing professional-grade photography to the masses. The 5MP macro lens adds versatility, allowing you to capture the minutiae of life with stunning clarity. The 32 MP selfie camera ensures that your personal moments are captured with the same level of detail.

The Evolution of Smartphone Technology

The journey of smartphone technology is a tale of relentless innovation and transformation. From the rudimentary Nokia 5120, which introduced mobile gaming to the masses, to the revolutionary iPhone that redefined user interaction with its touchscreen interface, smartphones have undergone a metamorphosis.

The last decade has witnessed the rise of open-source operating systems, bridging the gap between smartphones and laptops, and the introduction of foldable touchscreens. These advancements have paved the way for devices like the Ulefone

Note 17 Pro, which encapsulate the essence of modern smartphone technology.

Smartphones have transcended their original purpose as communication devices to become central hubs for our digital lives. They are now our wallets, cameras, libraries, and windows to the world. The Ulefone Note 17 Pro stands at the forefront of this evolution, driving the market forward with its innovative features and accessible pricing.

Chapter 1: Design and Display

The Art of Curved Oled

The Ulefone Note 17 Pro is not just a technological device; it's a masterpiece of modern design, epitomizing the art of curved OLED. In this section we will into the intricacies of curved OLED technology and how it enhances the user experience.

The Aesthetics of Curvature

Curved OLED displays represent the pinnacle of smartphone aesthetics. The gentle arc of the screen transforms the visual presentation into an immersive experience, extending beyond the flat confines of traditional displays. The Ulefone Note 17 Pro's OLED screen is a testament to this design philosophy, offering a seamless edge that draws the user into a vivid world of color and light.

Engineering Brilliance

The engineering behind the curved OLED is as impressive as its appearance. The flexibility of OLED technology allows for this curvature, which in turn contributes to the device's ergonomic feel. When held, the Ulefone Note 17 Pro's contours align naturally with the palm, making it not only a visual delight but also a comfortable fit for extended use.

Enhanced Interactivity

Curved screens are not merely about looks; they offer enhanced interactivity. The curvature allows for innovative features such as side notifications and edge controls, providing users with new ways to interact with their device. The Ulefone Note 17 Pro utilizes these possibilities to their fullest, offering a user experience that is intuitive and efficient.

Durability and Protection

Despite their sophisticated appearance, curved OLED screens are built to last. The Ulefone Note 17 Pro's display is protected by the latest advancements in scratch-resistant materials, ensuring that the beauty of the curved screen endures the rigors of daily use.

The curved OLED is more than just a component of the Ulefone Note 17 Pro; it is the soul of the device. It represents a harmonious blend of form and function, aesthetics and ergonomics, design and technology. This section has explored how the art of curved OLED elevates the smartphone experience, setting a new standard for what users can expect from their devices.

A New Era of Visual Experience

The Ulefone Note 17 Pro heralds a new era of visual experience, one that transcends the traditional boundaries of smartphone displays. In this section we will explore the transformative features that make the Note 17 Pro's display a marvel of modern technology.

Revolutionizing Resolution and Clarity

The Note 17 Pro's OLED display boasts a resolution that rivals the clarity of high-definition televisions. With a pixel density so high that the human eye cannot discern individual pixels, the screen presents images and videos with a level of detail that is nothing short of astonishing.

This leap in resolution marks a new chapter in the visual fidelity of handheld devices.

The Vibrancy of OLED Technology

OLED technology is renowned for its ability to deliver deep blacks and vibrant colors. The Note 17 Pro's display takes full advantage of this, offering a contrast ratio that makes every color pop and every shadow distinct. The result is a visual experience that is rich, dynamic, and incredibly immersive.

Curves That Captivate

The curved nature of the Note 17 Pro's display is not just a stylistic choice; it's a functional innovation. The curvature extends the display into the user's peripheral vision, creating a sense of depth and engagement that flat screens cannot match. This design choice is about more than aesthetics—it's about creating a more natural and comfortable viewing experience[3].

High Refresh Rates for Seamless Interaction

With a refresh rate of 120Hz, the Note 17 Pro's display offers a level of smoothness in motion that sets a new standard for mobile devices. Whether scrolling through web pages, playing graphics-intensive games, or watching fast-paced videos, the display maintains a fluidity that keeps up with the speed of life.

The Ulefone Note 17 Pro's display is not just a window to the digital world; it's a portal to a new dimension of visual experience. By pushing the limits of resolution, color, design, and interaction, the Note 17 Pro stands as a testament to the incredible potential of smartphone technology.

Ergonomics and Aesthetics

In the realm of smartphone design, ergonomics and aesthetics are not just complementary; they are deeply intertwined. This section will explore how the Ulefone Note 17 Pro embodies the perfect blend of these two essential design principles.

Ergonomics: The Science of Comfort

Ergonomics is the science that seeks to design products that fit the people who use them. For smartphones, this means creating a device that is comfortable to hold, easy to navigate, and intuitive to use[1]. The Ulefone Note 17 Pro has been meticulously crafted with these ergonomic principles in mind. Its curved edges and slim profile ensure that the phone fits comfortably in the hand, reducing strain during prolonged use. The placement of buttons and sensors is optimized for ease of reach, making the user experience as seamless as possible.

Aesthetics: The Art of Appeal

AESTHETICS, ON THE OTHER HAND, IS THE BRANCH OF PHILOSOPHY THAT DEALS WITH THE NATURE OF BEAUTY AND TASTE. In smartphone design, aesthetics is about creating a product that is not only functional but also visually appealing. The Ulefone Note 17 Pro's design is a testament to the aesthetic sensibilities of modern technology. Its sleek lines and minimalist approach speak to a design ethos that values simplicity and elegance. The vibrant OLED display serves as the centerpiece, drawing users in with its rich colors and deep contrasts.

Balancing Form and Function

The true artistry of smartphone design lies in balancing ergonomics and aesthetics. The Ulefone Note 17 Pro achieves this balance by ensuring that its stunning visual design does not compromise user comfort. The phone's contours are designed to align with the natural grip of the hand, while its visual interface is laid out to be both beautiful and user-friendly.

Innovation in Materials and Manufacturing

Advancements in materials and manufacturing have played a crucial role in the ergonomic and aesthetic design of the Ulefone Note 17 Pro. The use of lightweight, durable materials allows for a thinner, more elegant device without sacrificing strength or comfort. The precision manufacturing processes ensure that every curve and angle is crafted to perfection.

The Ulefone Note 17 Pro stands as a shining example of how ergonomics and aesthetics can coalesce to create a smartphone that is both a joy to use and a sight to behold.

Chapter 2: Performance Powerhouse

MediaTek Helio G99: The Heart of the Beast

At the core of the Ulefone Note 17 Pro's remarkable performance lies the MediaTek Helio G99 chipset, a marvel of modern processor technology. This section will dissect the capabilities of the Helio G99 and its crucial role in powering the Note 17 Pro.

The Octa-Core Configuration

The MediaTek Helio G99 is an octa-core chipset that features a dual-cluster architecture. It consists of two high-performance Cortex-A76 cores clocked at 2.2 GHz for demanding tasks and six power-efficient Cortex-A55 cores at 2.0 GHz for everyday usage. This configuration allows the Note 17 Pro to handle a wide range of tasks with ease, from high-definition gaming to multitasking between complex applications.

Manufacturing Prowess

The chipset is manufactured using a 6-nanometer process technology, which is a significant factor in its performance and efficiency. This advanced manufacturing process allows for a denser, more powerful chip that consumes less power, contributing to the Note 17 Pro's extended battery life and smooth performance.

Graphics and Gaming

The Helio G99 is equipped with a Mali-G57 MP2 GPU, which delivers robust graphics performance. It supports high frame rates and detailed textures, ensuring that games and other graphics-intensive applications run smoothly on the Note 17 Pro. The GPU's architecture is designed to optimize power consumption without compromising on visual quality, making it ideal for extended gaming sessions.

Memory and Storage

Supporting high-performance LPDDR4X memory up to 2,133MHz and fast UFS 2.2-class storage, the Helio G99 accelerates data access, maximizing performance in games, apps, and everyday activities. This means that the Note 17 Pro can quickly load apps, switch between them seamlessly, and store large amounts of data without slowing down.

Connectivity and Communication

While the Helio G99 does not support 5G, it offers comprehensive 4G LTE connectivity with Cat-13 download speeds. Additionally, it includes Wi-Fi 5 and Bluetooth 5.2, ensuring that the Note 17 Pro stays connected with fast and reliable wireless communication.

The MediaTek Helio G99 is the heart that pumps life into the Ulefone Note 17 Pro, driving its performance to new heights. It balances raw power with energy efficiency, enabling the Note 17 Pro to deliver a smooth, responsive user experience. This section has highlighted the technical prowess of the Helio G99, showcasing why it is the cornerstone of the Note 17 Pro's status as a performance powerhouse.

Ram and Storage: Speed Meets Capacity

In the world of smartphones, RAM (Random Access Memory) and storage are two critical components that determine a device's performance and user experience. This section will look into the significance of RAM and storage in the Ulefone Note 17 Pro, illustrating how they combine to create a powerhouse of speed and capacity.

Understanding RAM in Smartphones

RAM is the short-term memory of a smartphone, where the operating system, applications, and data in current use are stored for quick access. The more RAM a phone has, the more information it can store and access rapidly, which translates to faster app loading times, smoother multitasking, and an overall snappier performance. The Ulefone Note 17 Pro comes equipped with 12GB of LPDDR4X

RAM, which is on the higher end of the spectrum for 2024 smartphones. This generous amount of RAM allows for a seamless experience, even with multiple apps running simultaneously or when playing resource-intensive games.

The Role of Storage

Storage, on the other hand, is the long-term memory of the phone, used to store apps, photos, videos, and files. Unlike RAM, which is cleared when the phone is turned off, storage retains data even when the device is powered down. The Note 17 Pro features 256GB of UFS 2.2-class storage, providing ample space for all your needs and ensuring quick data retrieval and storage. This type of storage is known for its high read and write speeds, which contribute to the device's swift performance.

Speed Meets Capacity

The combination of 12GB of RAM and 256GB of storage in the Note 17 Pro means that users can enjoy the best of both worlds: speed and capacity. With this setup, the phone can handle everything from everyday tasks to the most demanding applications without breaking a sweat. Users can store a vast library of apps, photos, and videos, and switch between them effortlessly, thanks to the high-speed RAM.

Future-Proofing

In an era where smartphones are used for increasingly complex tasks, having a high amount of RAM and ample storage is essential for future-proofing a device. The Note 17 Pro's specifications ensure that it will remain competitive and capable of handling future software updates and more advanced apps that may require more memory and storage space.

RAM and storage are the unsung heroes of the smartphone experience. They work behind the scenes to ensure that the device operates at peak efficiency. The Ulefone Note 17 Pro's impressive RAM and storage capabilities are a testament to its status as a performance powerhouse, ready to take on the needs of any user, now and in the future.

Chapter 3: Photography Redefined

Capturing Moments with 108MP

The Ulefone Note 17 Pro's camera system is a testament to the incredible advancements in mobile photography. At the heart of this system is the 108MP main camera, a feature that redefines what we can capture with a smartphone. This section will explore the capabilities of this high-resolution camera and its impact on mobile photography.

The Power of 108 Megapixels

A 108MP camera represents a monumental leap in photographic detail and clarity. With a resolution of 108 million pixels, the camera captures images with a level of detail previously unseen in smartphone photography. This allows for stunningly clear photos that can be zoomed in or cropped without losing quality. The Ulefone Note 17 Pro utilizes this capability to deliver photos that are not just pictures but true representations of the moment captured.

Advanced Sensor Technology

The 108MP sensor on the Note 17 Pro is not just about the number of pixels; it's also about the quality of each pixel. The sensor size is 1/1.52", with a pixel size of 0.7μm, and it uses Phase Detection Auto Focus (PDAF) for quick and accurate focusing.

This advanced sensor technology ensures that each pixel captures more light and color information, resulting in vibrant and lifelike images.

High-Resolution Video Recording

Beyond still photography, the 108MP camera excels in video recording as well. It supports video resolutions up to 1440p at 30 frames per second, allowing users to capture their memories in high-definition[1]. This makes the Note 17 Pro not just a camera phone but a capable video recorder that can document life's moments with cinematic quality.

Pro-Grade Camera Features

The Ulefone Note 17 Pro's camera system comes equipped with features that cater to both amateur and professional photographers. It includes an LED flash, HDR, and panorama capabilities. These features give users the tools they need to take their photography to the next level, whether they're shooting landscapes, portraits, or action shots.

The 108MP camera of the Ulefone Note 17 Pro is more than just a feature; it's a gateway to a new era of mobile photography. It allows users to capture moments with unprecedented detail and clarity, making every photo a potential masterpiece. This section has detailed the technical prowess and creative potential of the Note 17 Pro's camera, showcasing it as a crucial feature that redefines the standards of smartphone photography.

Advanced Camera Features and Modes

The Ulefone Note 17 Pro's camera is not just about its 108MP sensor; it's also about the advanced features and modes that allow users to unleash their creativity and adapt to any photographic scenario. This section will detail these features and modes, highlighting how they contribute to the phone's versatile photography capabilities.

Manual/Pro Mode

Manual or Pro Mode gives photographers complete control over the camera settings. Users can adjust the shutter speed, ISO, white balance, and focus mode to suit their needs and the environment. This mode is ideal for those who understand the nuances of photography and wish to capture images with precise specifications.

Night Mode

Night Mode is designed for low-light conditions, utilizing a slow shutter speed to capture more light. This mode often requires a steady hand or a tripod to prevent blur, but the results are brighter, clearer images even in the darkest settings.

Pro Video

Pro Video extends the capabilities of Pro Mode to video recording, offering enhancements such as directional microphone control and the ability to adjust contrast, highlights, shadows, saturation, tint, and temperature. This mode is perfect for creating professional-quality videos with a smartphone.

Timelapse and Hyperlapse

Timelapse and Hyperlapse modes allow users to capture the passage of time in a creative way. Timelapse uses a series of photos taken at set intervals to create a fast-forward video effect, while Hyperlapse is based on video footage and offers adjustable speed settings.

Slow-motion Video

Slow-motion video mode captures fast-paced action by increasing the number of frames per second (fps). The higher the fps, the slower the motion appears in the video, allowing users to observe details that would otherwise be missed.

Portrait/Bokeh/Live Focus

Portrait mode, also known as Bokeh or Live Focus, blurs the background while keeping the subject in sharp focus. This mode creates a depth-of-field effect that emphasizes the subject and adds a professional look to portraits.

RAW Images

Shooting in RAW format captures the maximum data from the image sensor, providing photographers with a greater range of editing possibilities. This format is preferred by professionals who require high-quality images for post-processing.

Customized Modes

In addition to the standard modes, smartphone manufacturers often include customized modes tailored to their devices. These can include UltraShot HDR, Nightscape, AR Stickers, 3D SoundTracking, AI Beauty, and more, each designed to enhance specific types of photography.

The advanced camera features and modes of the Ulefone Note 17 Pro empower users to explore the full potential of mobile photography. Whether capturing the night sky, recording a child's first steps in slow motion, or shooting a professional portrait, the Note 17 Pro's camera adapts to the user's vision, making it a versatile tool for any photographic endeavor.

Chapter 4: User Experience

Navigating Android 13

The user experience of a smartphone is largely defined by its operating system. With the Ulefone Note 17 Pro running on Android 13, users are treated to a suite of features that enhance usability, customization, and overall interaction with the device. This section will provide a detailed exploration of navigating Android

13 and the user-centric innovations it brings to the Note 17 Pro.

Intuitive Interface and Customization

Android 13 continues the legacy of its predecessor's Material You design, offering a more personalized and intuitive interface[1]. Users can enjoy auto-theming icons that align with the system's color palette, providing a cohesive and aesthetically pleasing look across the entire UI[1]. The addition of six new color palettes in Android 13 allows for even more customization, catering to the user's preference for specific shades or complementary hues.

Enhanced Launcher Search

The improved launcher search feature in Android 13 is a significant upgrade, making it easier for users to find apps, contacts, and information quickly. The search bar at the bottom of the home screen now provides web results as well as app-related content, streamlining the process of locating what you need.

Privacy and Security Enhancements

Android 13 places a strong emphasis on privacy and security, giving users more control over their data. The operating system includes updated permissions settings that allow users to grant or deny access to sensitive information on a per-app basis. This ensures that personal data is protected and only shared with trusted applications.

Improved Notifications and QR Code Scanning

Notifications have been refined in Android 13, offering a cleaner and more organized way to view important alerts. Quick access to QR code scanning is another practical addition, enabling users to interact with QR codes from the lock screen or notification shade swiftly.

Language Preferences and Battery Information

One of the standout features of Android 13 is the ability to set per-app language preferences, allowing users to choose different languages for individual apps without changing the system language[3]. Additionally, the OS provides better battery information, helping users understand their device's power consumption and manage battery life more effectively.

Navigating Android 13 on the Ulefone Note 17 Pro is a seamless and enjoyable experience. The operating system's focus on customization, ease of use, and privacy makes it an ideal platform for the modern smartphone user. This section has detailed the key features and improvements that Android 13 offers, highlighting how they contribute to the superior user experience on the Note 17 Pro.

Customization and Control

The Ulefone Note 17 Pro, powered by Android 13, offers a rich tapestry of customization and control options that put the user firmly in the driver's seat. This section will look into the myriad ways users can tailor their experience to their liking, showcasing the flexibility and power of Android 13.

Personalization at Your Fingertips

Android 13 introduces a new level of personalization, allowing users to customize their devices to reflect their style and preferences. With dynamic color theming, the system can extract dominant, complementary colors from the user's wallpaper to theme the entire UI, including notification shades, lock screens, and volume controls. This feature extends to app icons, ensuring a uniform and visually appealing interface.

Control Over Privacy

Privacy is paramount in Android 13, and users have granular control over what data they share and with whom. The operating system provides the option to share only specific photos with an app, rather than granting access to the entire gallery. Additionally, users can control how and when apps access their location, providing peace of mind and enhanced security.

Language Preferences

In a multilingual world, the ability to set language preferences for each app is a game-changer. Android 13 allows users to choose different languages for individual apps, catering to the diverse linguistic needs of global users. This feature is particularly useful for those who prefer to use certain apps in their native language while keeping the system language different.

Accessibility and Ease of Use

Android 13 makes the device more accessible and easier to use. The operating system includes features like button navigation to enable Google Assistant, simplifying the interaction for users who prefer traditional navigation methods. Moreover, users can control smart home devices directly from the lock screen without unlocking the phone, adding convenience to everyday tasks.

Customized Notifications and Clock

Users can customize how they view notifications and even the lock screen clock. Android 13 offers the ability to disable the double-line clock on the lock screen, providing more space for notifications and a cleaner look. The notification system itself is more streamlined, with categorized alerts that make it easier to manage incoming information.

Customization and control are the cornerstones of the Android 13 experience on the Ulefone Note 17 Pro. The operating system empowers users to shape their mobile experience to suit their individual needs and preferences. This section has detailed the extensive customization options and the robust control features that Android 13 offers, illustrating why it stands out as a user-centric platform.

Chapter 5: Ahead of the Curve

Innovations in Battery and Charging

The Ulefone Note 17 Pro distinguishes itself with state-of-the-art battery technology and charging capabilities, setting a new standard for endurance and convenience. This section will look into the innovations that place the Note 17 Pro ahead of the curve in battery and charging technology.

High-Density Battery Technology

The Note 17 Pro is powered by a high-density lithium polymer battery, which offers a significant increase in energy storage capacity without adding bulk. This technology allows for a slimmer design while providing extended battery life, enabling users to go longer between charges.

Ultra-Fast Charging

Charging speed is a critical aspect of the user experience, and the Note 17 Pro excels with its ultra-fast charging capability. The device supports a rapid charging protocol that can charge the battery to 50% in just 20 minutes, ensuring that users can quickly power up and get on with their day.

Wireless Charging Convenience

Wireless charging has become a must-have feature for flagship phones, and the Note 17 Pro includes this convenient option. It allows users to charge their device by simply placing it on a compatible charging pad, eliminating the need for cables and providing a clutter-free charging experience.

Reverse Wireless Charging

In addition to standard wireless charging, the Note 17 Pro supports reverse wireless charging, enabling it to share power with other devices. This feature turns the phone into a portable charging station, capable of wirelessly charging compatible accessories or even another phone.

Smart Charging Algorithms

The Note 17 Pro employs smart charging algorithms that optimize the charging process to extend the battery's lifespan. These algorithms monitor the battery's temperature and charging speed, adjusting them in real-time to prevent overheating and reduce wear and tear.

Energy-Efficient Display and Processor

Complementing the battery innovations, the Note 17 Pro's OLED display and efficient MediaTek Helio G99 processor contribute to overall energy savings. The display uses less power than traditional LCDs, and the processor is designed to maximize performance without excessive power consumption.

The Ulefone Note 17 Pro's innovations in battery and charging technology are a testament to the brand's commitment to pushing the boundaries of what's possible. From its high-density battery to its ultra-fast and wireless charging capabilities, the Note 17 Pro ensures that users can stay connected and productive without constant concerns about battery life.

Connectivity and Communication

In the digital age, connectivity and communication are the lifeblood of technology, shaping how we interact with the world and each other. The Ulefone Note 17 Pro, with its advanced features, stands as a testament to these crucial aspects of modern life. This section will explore the various facets of connectivity and communication that the Note 17 Pro offers.

Cellular Networks: The Backbone of Communication

The Note 17 Pro supports the latest 4G LTE standards, providing users with fast and reliable mobile data connectivity. This allows for high-speed internet access on the go, ensuring that users can browse, stream, and download content with ease. The phone's ability to switch seamlessly between different network bands enhances coverage and connection stability, even in areas with weak signal strength.

Wi-Fi: High-Speed Wireless Internet

Wi-Fi connectivity is essential for accessing high-speed internet without using cellular data. The Note 17 Pro supports Wi-Fi 6, the latest standard that offers increased speed, improved range, and better performance in crowded areas. This ensures that users can enjoy a fast and stable internet connection while at home, work, or public hotspots.

Bluetooth: Short-Range Wireless Technology

Bluetooth technology enables the Note 17 Pro to connect with a wide range of devices, from headphones and speakers to wearables and car systems. The phone features Bluetooth 5.2, which provides faster transfer speeds, longer range, and the ability to connect multiple devices simultaneously.

NFC: Simplifying Transactions and Pairing

Near Field Communication (NFC) is a feature that allows for contactless payments and easy pairing with compatible devices. With NFC, the Note 17 Pro users can make secure transactions with a simple tap, streamlining the checkout process in stores and enabling quick connections with other NFC-enabled devices.

USB-C: Universal Charging and Data Transfer

The Note 17 Pro comes with a USB-C port, which has become the standard for charging and data transfer. USB-C offers faster charging and data transfer rates, and its reversible design makes it more convenient to use.

Connectivity and communication are at the heart of the Ulefone Note 17 Pro's design philosophy. The device integrates a multitude of technologies to ensure that users remain connected to the digital world and to each other. From cellular networks to Wi-Fi, Bluetooth, NFC, and USB-C, the Note 17 Pro is equipped to handle the diverse needs of modern smartphone users, keeping them ahead of the curve in an ever-connected world.

Chapter 6: Market Impact

Competing in the Flagship Arena

The Ulefone Note 17 Pro's entry into the smartphone market is a bold move, positioning itself as a mid-range device with flagship aspirations. This section will analyze its market impact and how it competes in the flagship arena.

A Mid-Range Contender with Flagship Features

The Note 17 Pro brings to the table an impressive array of features typically reserved for higher-end models. With a 108MP main camera, a curved AMOLED display, and the MediaTek Helio G99 processor, it offers a compelling package for its price point. However, priced at 300 euros, it enters a fiercely competitive market segment where it must prove its value against established brands and their offerings.

Design and Display: Standing Out

The device makes a striking first impression with its design and display technology. The 6.78-inch 120Hz AMOLED curved display sets it apart in the mid-range market, offering a premium feel that could attract users looking for high-end aesthetics at a lower cost.

Performance: Balancing Cost and Capabilities

Powered by the Helio G99 processor and equipped with 12GB of RAM and 256GB of storage, the Note 17 Pro promises smooth performance for everyday tasks and multitasking. While it may not support the latest 5G connectivity, its 4G LTE capabilities and Wi-Fi 6 support ensure that it remains a viable option for users who do not prioritize 5G.

Photography: High-Resolution at a Lower Price

The 108MP main camera is a standout feature that positions the Note 17 Pro as a strong contender for mobile photography enthusiasts. This high-resolution camera, combined with a 32 MP front camera and a 5MP macro lens, provides users with a versatile photography experience.

Battery and Charging: Keeping Pace with Demand

The Note 17 Pro's 5050mAh battery and 33W wired charging capability align it with current market expectations for battery life and charging speed. While it may not offer the fastest charging available, it provides a balance between performance and cost.

Market Reception: A Mixed Bag

Since its release, the Note 17 Pro has received mixed reviews. While it impresses with its specifications and design, it faces stiff competition from other mid-range devices that offer similar or better features. Its success in the market will depend on how well it can differentiate itself and appeal to consumers looking for a balance between price and performance.

The Ulefone Note 17 Pro's market impact is defined by its ability to offer flagship-like features at a mid-range price. As it competes in the flagship arena, its success will hinge on its ability to convince consumers that it can provide a premium experience without the premium price tag. This section has explored the various factors that contribute to the Note 17 Pro's position in the market, highlighting its strengths and the challenges it faces.

Consumer Reception and Reviews

The Ulefone Note 17 Pro has garnered attention in the smartphone market, eliciting a range of opinions from users and reviewers. Here's a detailed look at the reception and reviews it has received:

User Opinions

Users have expressed mixed feelings about the Ulefone Note 17 Pro. Some appreciate its design and the inclusion of a curved screen, which is a departure from Ulefone's typical rugged phone style. However, there are concerns about the practicality of finding suitable screen protectors for the curved display. Others question the brand's shift towards a more conventional smartphone, pondering if it can truly compete with established names in the industry.

Professional Reviews

Reviewers acknowledge the Ulefone Note 17 Pro's beautiful design and impressive specifications, such as the 108MP camera and the Helio G99 processor. Despite these features, some reviews suggest that the phone may not be competitive enough in terms of pricing when compared to other devices in the same segment. The consensus seems to be that while the Note 17 Pro has potential, its success hinges on whether it can distinguish itself in a crowded market.

Overall Impact

The Ulefone Note 17 Pro's market impact is somewhat mixed. It has certainly made waves with its high-resolution camera and curved display, but it faces the challenge of proving its value against more established competitors. The device's reception will likely evolve as more users get their hands on it and as Ulefone continues to navigate the competitive landscape of mid-range smartphones.

Chapter 7: The Future is Flexible

Predictions for Next-Gen Smartphones

The smartphone industry is on the cusp of a new era, with next-generation devices poised to redefine our understanding of mobile technology. This section will explore the predictions for next-gen smartphones, drawing from industry insights and technological trends.

Holographic Displays and Accessories

One of the most anticipated features is the integration of holographic displays, which could revolutionize the way we interact with our devices. These displays would allow for three-dimensional visuals without the need for special glasses, making gaming, video calls, and content consumption more immersive than ever before.

Universal Wireless Charging

The future may also see the widespread adoption of universal wireless charging, enabling smartphones to be charged from a distance and without the need for specific charging pads. This would add a new level of convenience and flexibility to device charging.

Enhanced AI and Machine Learning Capabilities

Artificial Intelligence (AI) and Machine Learning (ML) are set to become even more integral to smartphones. Next-gen devices are expected to feature SoCs capable of running on-device Generative AI (GenAI) models more quickly and efficiently, leveraging neural processing units (NPUs) with significant performance improvements. This could lead to features like real-time translation during calls, advanced photo editing suites, and even AI-generated content creation.

5G Connectivity and Beyond

While 5G is already being rolled out, future smartphones will likely expand on this technology, offering more robust connectivity options and functionality. This could include improved network stability, faster data speeds, and new services that leverage the high bandwidth of 5G networks.

Longer-Lasting Battery Life

Battery technology is also expected to advance, with predictions pointing towards longer-lasting batteries that could provide days of usage on a single charge. This would be a significant improvement over current battery life standards.

'Remote Control' Capabilities

Smartphones may evolve to become the central 'remote control' for our lives, managing everything from smart home devices to personal health data. The rise of superapps could consolidate many functions into single, multifunctional applications.

Health-Tracking Innovations

Health-tracking technology is predicted to see innovations, with smartphones playing a key role in monitoring and managing health-related data. This could include more accurate sensors and integration with medical devices.

The future of smartphones is indeed flexible, with predictions pointing towards a range of exciting developments. From holographic displays to AI-driven features and health-tracking innovations, next-gen smartphones are set to transform the mobile landscape. This section has provided a glimpse into what we can expect from the smartphones of tomorrow, highlighting the potential for these devices to become even more integrated into our daily lives.

The Role of Ulefone in Shaping Technology

Ulefone has established itself as a significant player in the mobile technology sector, particularly known for producing high-quality mobile devices and accessories. The company's impact on technology can be seen in several key areas:

Quality and Affordability

Ulefone has been recognized for manufacturing smartphones that balance quality and affordability. By leveraging high-tech manufacturing processes and maintaining strict quality control, Ulefone has minimized defect rates in its products. This commitment to quality, coupled with competitive pricing due to large-scale production, has allowed Ulefone to offer cost-effective devices to consumers.

Customer Support and Firmware Updates

The company places a strong emphasis on customer support and frequently updates its firmware, ensuring that customers receive reliable software updates and security patches. This approach helps in building customer trust and loyalty, as users feel supported throughout the lifespan of their devices.

Diverse Product Range

With a wide range of products, Ulefone caters to various consumer needs and preferences. Whether customers are looking for rugged phones, conventional smartphones, or accessories, Ulefone strives to provide options that satisfy different market segments.

Innovation and Adaptability

Ulefone's move to introduce devices like the Note 17 Pro with a curved OLED display and high-resolution cameras indicates the company's adaptability and willingness to innovate. By incorporating features typically found in flagship models, Ulefone is contributing to the democratization of advanced mobile technology, making it accessible to a broader audience.

Global Presence

Ulefone's impact extends beyond its home market, with a growing number of users worldwide. The company's ability to meet international standards and consumer expectations has helped it carve out a space in the global market. Ulefone's role in shaping technology is marked by its dedication to quality, customer service, and innovation. By offering a diverse product lineup and staying responsive to market trends, Ulefone continues to influence the mobile device industry and contribute to technological advancements.

Conclusion

The Note 17 Pro in the Pantheon of Phones The Ulefone Note 17 Pro has carved out its niche in the pantheon of modern smartphones. It stands as a testament to Ulefone's commitment to innovation and consumer value. With its curved OLED display, high-resolution camera, and robust performance, the Note 17 Pro challenges the status quo, offering features once exclusive to high-end models at a more accessible price point. It represents a shift in the market dynamics, where quality and advanced features become available to a wider audience, potentially reshaping consumer expectations and demands.

Final Thoughts on the OLED Revolution

The OLED revolution has been a game-changer in the smartphone industry, and the Note 17 Pro is a part of this transformative journey. OLED technology has enabled thinner, more energy-efficient displays with superior color accuracy and contrast ratios. As this technology becomes more prevalent, it paves the way for further innovations such as foldable screens and more immersive visual experiences. The Note 17 Pro's adoption of OLED is a clear indicator that Ulefone is not just following trends but is keen on being at the forefront, pushing the boundaries of what's possible in smartphone technology.

The Ulefone Note 17 Pro, with its blend of style, functionality, and affordability, is a significant player in the ongoing evolution of mobile devices. It encapsulates the spirit of the OLED revolution, marking a step towards a future where cutting-edge technology is not just a luxury but a standard for all.

Thank you for your purchase of this book. Your support to me means a lot, and I hope that you find it an informative and absorbing reading.

But if you have time, I'd appreciate your writing a review. With your response, I can be better and help other readers.

Thank you once more for your assistance, and best _ wishes on your journey.

www.ingramcontent.com/pod-product-compliance
Lightning Source LLC
Chambersburg PA
CBHW070411230526
45471CB00006B/2759